Table of Contents

D1710490

The Mole Family

A floor plan shows where things are placed in a room. The Mole Family has just had all of their new living room furniture delivered. Now they have to arrange it. Help them decide where to put each piece of furniture. Color and cut out the pictures of the furniture. Glue the pictures on the drawing of the Mole Family's living room to make a floor plan.

Mole Family's Floor Plan

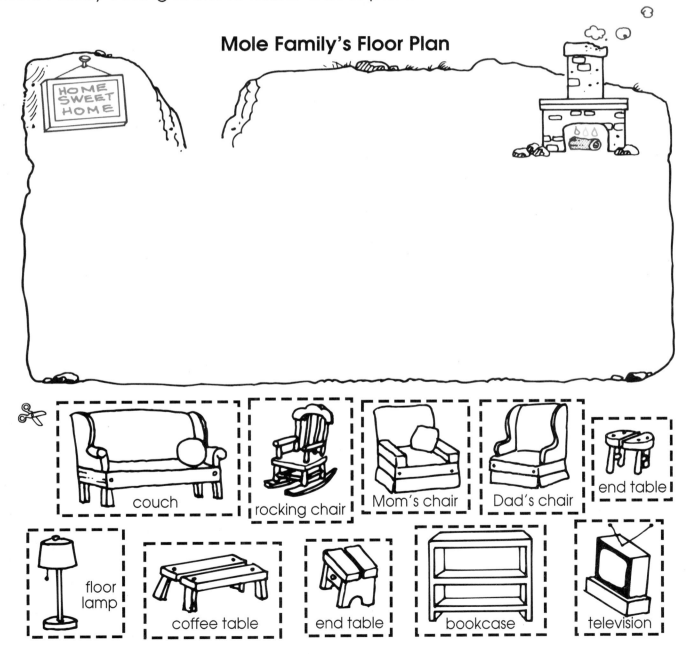

This page has been
intentionally left blank.

A Picture From Above

A floor plan looks like a picture someone drew looking down from the sky.
It shows you where things are.

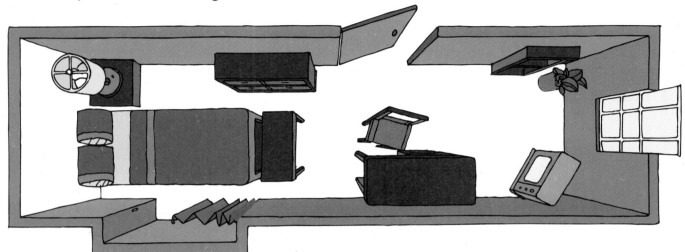

Circle the word which correctly completes each statement.

1. The TV is near the…   a. door   b. window   c. bed
2. The dresser is near the…   a. window   b. door   c. TV
3. Next to the bed is a…   a. TV   b. window   c. table
4. The bench is at the end of the… a. bed   b. bookshelf   c. closet
5. The plant is by the…   a. dresser   b. bed   c. bookshelf
6. The bookshelf is next to the… a. bed   b. closet   c. door
7. The lamp is on the…   a. table   b. TV   c. dresser

Follow these directions.

1. Draw a red circle around the TV.
2. Draw a black **X** on the desk.
3. Draw an oval rug in front of the bench using a color of your choice.
4. Draw a stuffed animal in the center of the bed.

Fill in these blanks with the correct word.

1. Between the closet and the TV is a _____.

2. The window is between the _____ and the TV.

3. When you walk in the door, the _____ is to your right.

4. There is/are _____ lamp(s) in the room.

Name: _____

Prepare for the Show

It's the big event of the year! Old cars from all over the United States are being put on display. The boxes on the floor plan show the spaces where cars will be placed. Follow the directions on page 7 to complete the floor plan.

Car Display Floor Plan

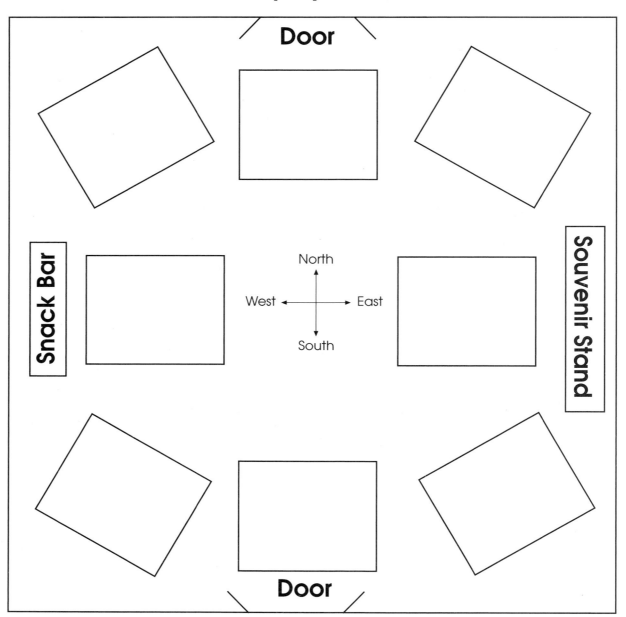

Name: _____

Prepare for the Show

Color and cut out the pictures of the cars at the bottom of the page. Read the directions below to glue the pictures where they belong on page 6.

Directions:

1. The station wagon is in the space near the north door.

2. The roadster is in the space near the south door.

3. The van is in the space east of the station wagon.

4. The pickup is in the space west of the roadster.

5. The coupe is in the space west of the station wagon.

6. The carriage is in the space east of the roadster and south of the Souvenir Stand.

7. The Model A is east of the Snack Bar.

8. The Model T is east of the Model A.

station wagon

roadster

van

pickup

coupe

carriage

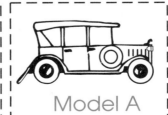
Model A

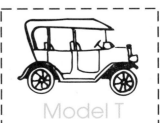
Model T

This page has been
intentionally left blank.

Name: _____

Hannah's New House

Hannah's family just moved into a new house. It is very different from their other house. Hannah drew a floor plan of her new house. Use the floor plan to answer the questions here and on page 10.

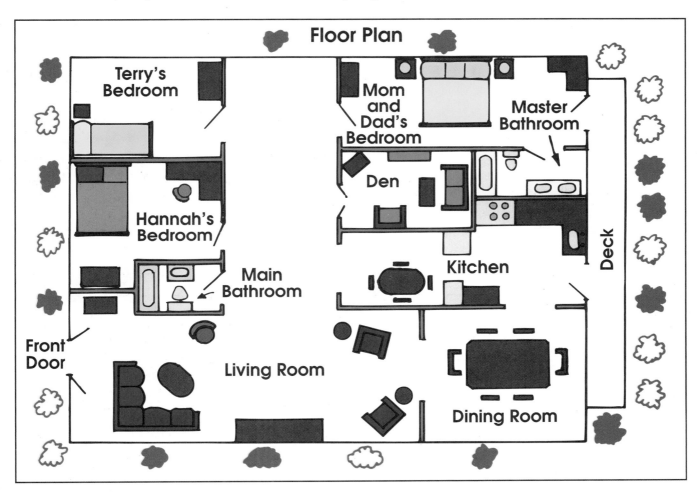

1. How many rooms does the house have? _____

2. Which room is the smallest? _____

3. Which room is the largest? _____

Hannah's New House

4. Who has a room across from Mom and Dad's bedroom?

_____

5. Which rooms does Hannah walk past to go from the living room to her own bedroom?

_____

6. How many bedrooms are there? _____

7. Which rooms have a door leading onto the deck?

_____

8. The front door opens into what room?

_____

9. On the floor plan on page 9, use a red crayon to draw the routes Hannah could take from her room to a door leading outside in case of an emergency.

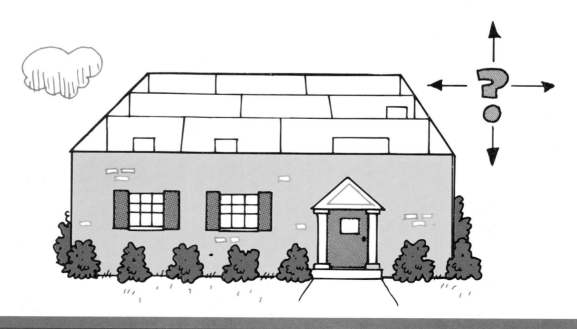

Name: _____

Symbols on Maps

A symbol is a picture that stands for something that is shown on a map. Symbols used in a map are shown in the Map Key. Look at the symbols. Draw a line from each symbol to what it stands for in the drawing below.

Map Key

Name: _____

Symbols Replace Words

Symbols on a map show you where things are located.

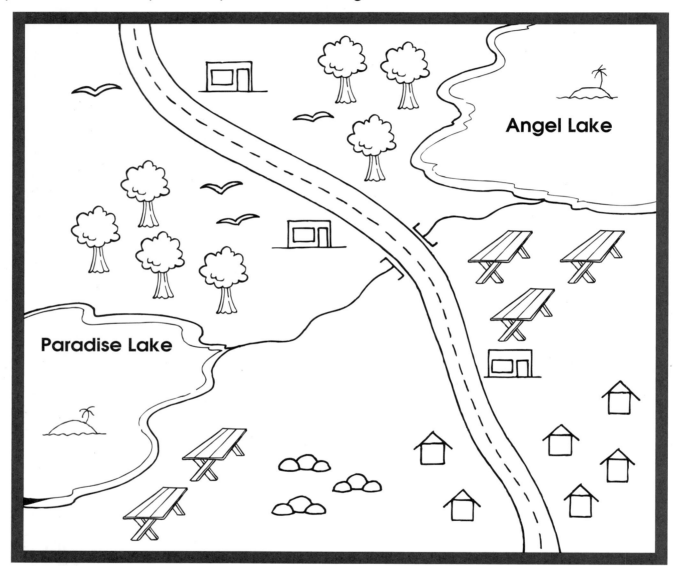

Directions: Use crayons or markers to complete the map.

1. Color the islands brown.
2. Color the trees green.
3. Color the rocks black.
4. Color the houses blue.
5. Color the stores orange.
6. Color the birds purple.
7. Color the picnic tables red.
8. Color the road yellow.

Name: _____

Kool Kids Mall

Mall Map

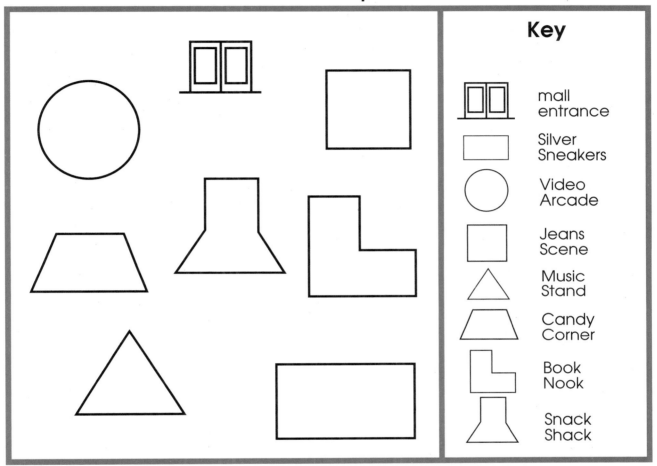

Directions: Use the key to locate the stores. Draw the following:

1. a red and blue sneaker in Silver Sneakers
2. a black musical note in the Music Stand
3. a pair of blue jeans in the Jeans Scene
4. a green tree on each side of the mall entrance
5. a red piece of pizza in the Snack Shack
6. a pair of eyes in the Video Arcade
7. a yellow book and a blue book in the Book Nook
8. an orange lollipop in the Candy Corner

Farmer Fritz

Map symbols can tell us how many of something there are. Each symbol can stand for 1 or any number of that item. This map shows Farmer Fritz's crops. Each vegetable or fruit stands for 1 plant. Use the map and key to answer the questions.

Garden Map   **Key**

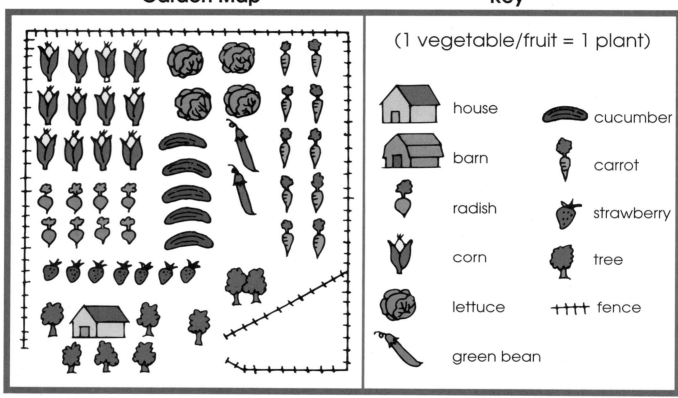

1. How many plants of each vegetable does Farmer Fritz have?

   radish _____   cucumber _____   corn _____

   carrot _____   green bean_____   lettuce_____

2. What fruit did Farmer Fritz plant?_____

   How many of these plants did he have? _____

3. Farmer Fritz planted the most of which vegetable? _____

Carmella's Candy

Carmella made a map of her candy store so that her customers could easily find their favorite candy. Use the map and key to answer the questions.

Candy Store Map

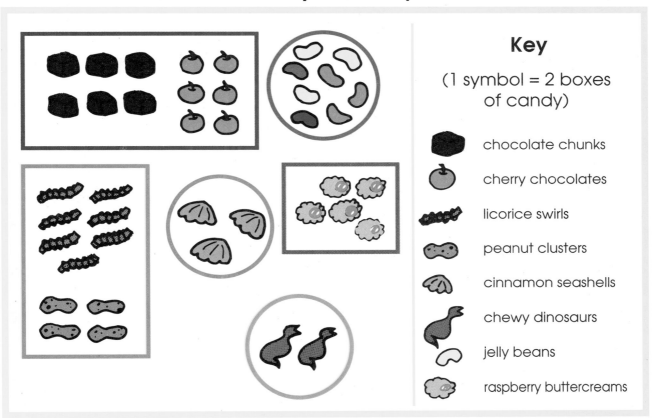

1. Each symbol equals how many boxes of candy? _____

2. How many boxes of each kind of candy are there?

jelly beans	_____	licorice swirls	_____
chocolate chunks	_____	cherry chocolates	_____
peanut clusters	_____	chewy dinosaurs	_____
raspberry buttercreams	_____	cinnamon seashells	_____

3. Carmella has the greatest number of boxes of which candy?

_____

Name: _____

Take a Hike

This is a map showing three hiking trails.

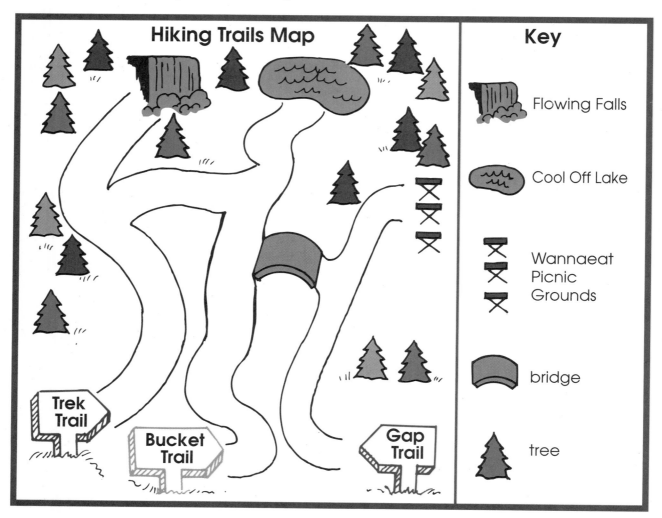

Directions:

1. Draw a red line along the trail that leads to the Wannaeat Picnic Grounds.

2. Draw a yellow line along the trail that leads to Flowing Falls.

3. Draw a green line along the trail that leads to Cool Off Lake.

4. Draw a blue line to show how you can go from Trek Trail to Cool Off Lake.

5. Draw an orange line to show how you can go from Bucket Trail to the Wannaeat Picnic Grounds.

Name: _____

Going from Place to Place

Some maps show you where places are located in a town.

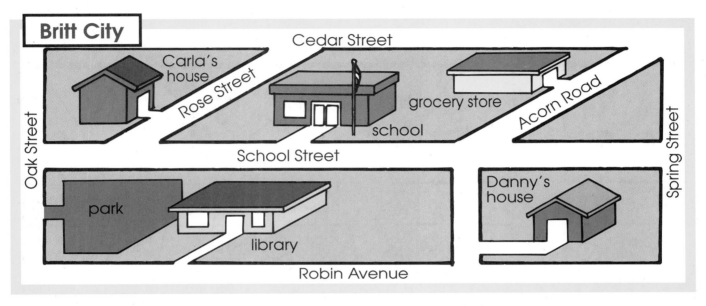

Circle the word that tells which is **closest** to Danny's house.

1. Carla's house   OR   the library
2. Robin Avenue   OR   Oak Street
3. the park   OR   the grocery store
4. Spring Street   OR   Cedar Street

Circle the word that tells which is **farthest** from Carla's house.

1. Spring Street   OR   Rose Street
2. the park   OR   Danny's house
3. the school   OR   the library
4. Oak Street   OR   Acorn Road

Add the following items to the map of Britt City.

1. Draw a flower garden on the corner of Spring Street and Robin Avenue.
2. Draw a swimming pool behind Carla's house.
3. Draw a baseball or football field behind the school.
4. Draw a car in front of Carla's house.
5. Draw a school bus on School Street.
6. Use a red crayon to draw the shortest path from Carla's house to Danny's.

Victory Celebration

Betsy, Rachel and Pat were so happy! They won their first baseball game. To celebrate, they wanted to have pizza and ice cream. Use this map and key to complete page 19.

Map

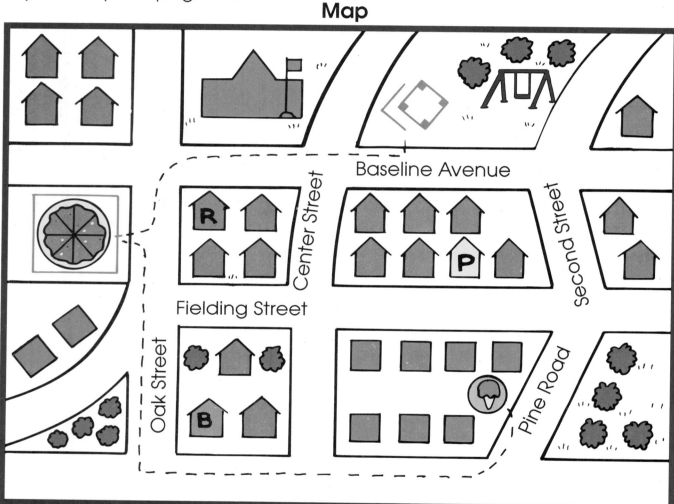

Key

- - - - route
baseball field
park
ice-cream shop
tree

school
store
pizza parlor
Betsy's house

house
Rachel's house
Pat's house

Victory Celebration

1. Use your finger to follow the route the girls took from the baseball field to the pizza parlor. On what street did they walk when they first left the baseball field?

   _____

2. Did they walk past the school? _____

3. Did they walk past a park? _____

4. On what street is the pizza parlor? _____

5. Use your finger to trace their route to the ice-cream shop. On what street is the ice-cream shop?

   _____

6. Then, it was time to go home. Use a blue crayon to mark a route Betsy might have taken home.

7. Use a red crayon to mark a route Rachel might have taken home.

8. Use a purple crayon to mark a route Pat might have taken home.

The Compass Rose

This is a compass rose. It tells the directions on a map. There are four arrows. Each arrow points in a different direction. These are called **cardinal** directions.

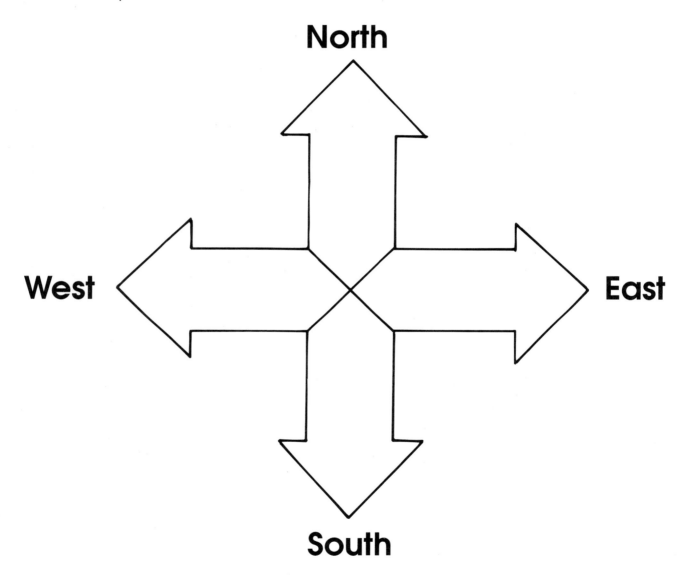

North

West

East

South

1. The arrow that points up is **north**. Color it blue.

2. The arrow that points down is **south**. Color it red.

3. The arrow that points to the right is **east**. Color it green.

4. The arrow that points to the left is **west**. Color it brown.

Name: _____

Pirate's Booty

Sedgewick the Pirate must be able to find his buried treasure when he returns to the island. Read the sentences. Write the words **north**, **south**, **east** and **west** in the blanks to help Sedgewick locate his treasure. Use the compass rose to help you.

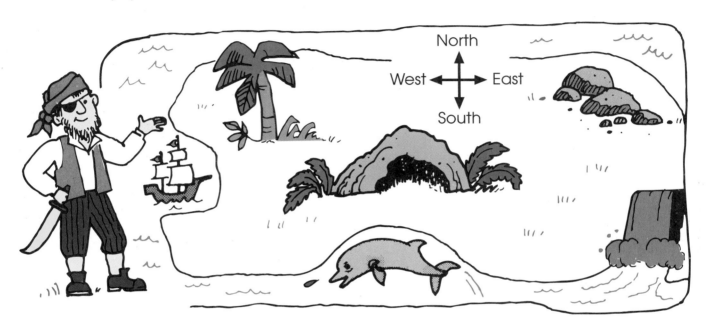

1. Dock the ship on the_____ side of the island.

2. Walk_____ to the cave.

3. Then, walk_____ to Dolphin Cove.

4. Go _____ to the waterfall.

5. Go_____ to the rocks.

6. Then, go_____ to the palm tree.

7. Draw an **X** below the palm tree to show where the treasure is buried.

Name: _____

What Do Hikers See?

Follow the directions to complete this area map.

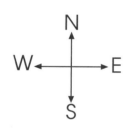

1. Draw a 🌊 west of the ⛰️ .

2. Draw 6 🌲 south of the 🌊 .

3. Draw an 🏝️ in the middle of the 🌊 .

4. Draw 10 ⛺ south of the ⛰️ .

5. Draw a 〰️ between the ⛰️ and the 🌊 .

6. Draw 2 ⛵ on the east side of the 🌊 .

7. Draw 2 🏠 south of the 6 🌲 .

8. Draw 3 🧍 south of the ⛺ .

Name: _____

Dizzy Designers

Decorate the compass rose boxes by following the directions below.

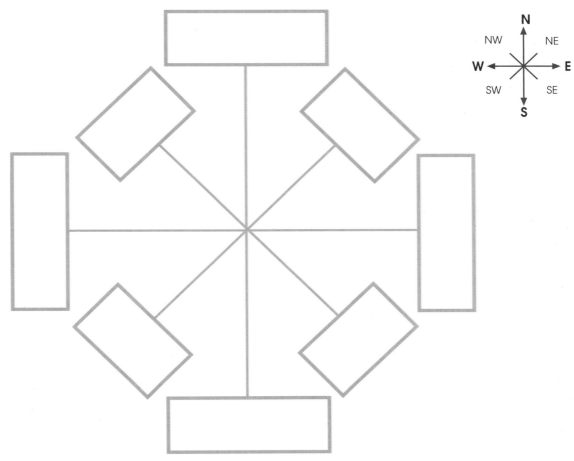

1. Draw red and black stripes in the **SW** box.

2. Draw 3 green triangles in the **N** box.

3. Make the **E** box red and blue plaid.

4. Draw purple polka dots in the **NW** box.

5. Make orange wavy lines in the **SE** box.

6. Draw two red squares in the **S** box.

7. Draw green diagonal lines in the **W** box.

8. Make two yellow smiling faces in the **NE** box.

Name: _____

Space Ship Search

Gus Galactic needs help in identifying these alien spaceships. Write a ship's letter in each blank to solve these riddles.

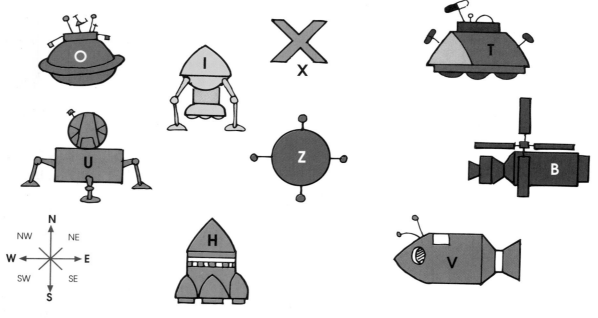

1. I am **N** of Ship **H**. _____
2. I am **E** of Ship **Z**. _____
3. I am **SE** of Ship **Z**. _____
4. I am **S** of Ship **O**. _____
5. I am **NW** of Ship **Z**. _____

6. I am **SW** of Ship **B**. _____
7. I am **NE** of Ship **Z**. _____
8. I am **NE** of Ship **I**. _____
9. I am **SE** of Ship **U**. _____
10. I am **NW** of Ship **B**. _____

Cosmic Challenge

Start at Ship H. Travel in the orbit given. Which ship will you dock with?

1. Go **NW** to Ship _____.
2. Go **NE** to Ship _____.
3. Go **NE** to Ship _____.
4. Go **S** to Ship _____.

5. Go **SE** to Ship _____.
6. Go **NE** to Ship _____.
7. Go **NW** to Ship _____.

This is your docking station. Congratulations!

Name: _____

Draw Your Own Map

A cartographer makes maps. Try your hand at being a cartographer and make your own map by following these directions. Read all directions before you begin.

1. Draw a compass rose using both cardinal and intermediate directions in the bottom right-hand corner of the map.
2. Draw a lake in the center of the map.
3. Northwest of the lake, draw some ducks in flight.
4. Directly south of the lake, draw six trees.
5. East of the ducks, draw the sun.
6. Southwest of the lake, draw a playground area.
7. East of the lake, draw a picnic area.

Name: _____

Legends Help You Read Maps

A legend is another word for a key. A map legend explains the symbols found in a map.

Star City

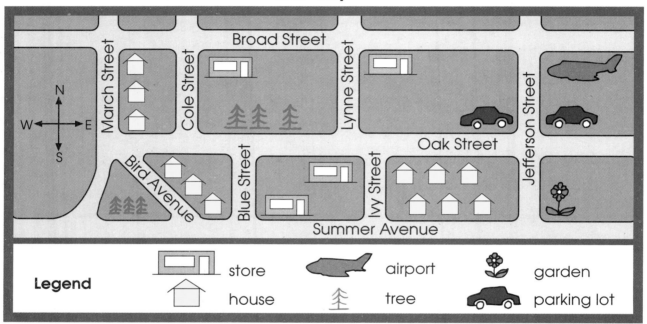

Directions: Use the legend box to answer the questions.

1. Does Star City have an airport? _____

2. How many houses are on Bird Avenue? _____

3. What is on the corner of Oak Street and Jefferson Street? _____

4. The garden is on the corner of Jefferson Street and _____.

5. How many stores are in Star City? _____

6. What direction is Summer Avenue from Oak Street? _____

7. Which street is directly west of Ivy Street? _____

8. How many trees are north of Oak Street? _____

9. How many houses are between Ivy Street and Jefferson Street? _____

10. How many stores are north of Summer Avenue? _____

Name: _____

Tourist Map of Oldtown

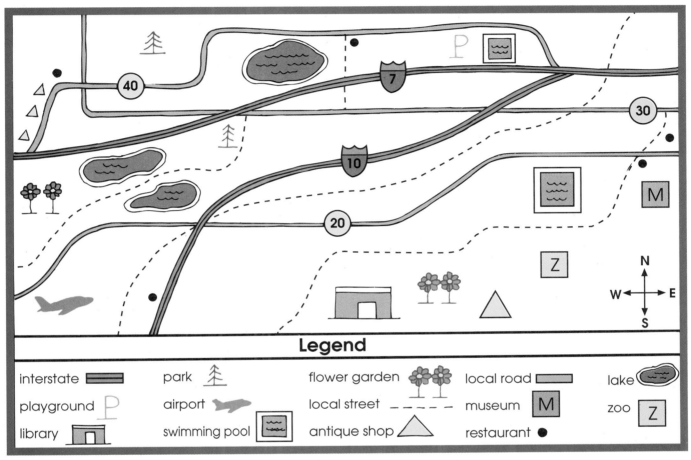

1. The airport is located between interstate_____and local road_____.

2. What attractions are north of interstate 7? _____

   _____

3. Could you take a local street from the airport to the library? _____

4. How many lakes are in Oldtown? _____

5. On which side of town is the museum located? _____

6. What is located at the point where local road 30 crosses interstate 7? _____

7. Name the road that runs north of the playground. _____

8. How many swimming pools are in Oldtown? _____

9. How many antique shops are in the town? _____

10. Is there a local street between the zoo and the swimming pool? _____

Name: _____

North, South, East and West

You are flying in an airplane with the wind blowing sharply in your face. You are flying from Chicago to Nashville. In what direction are you traveling?

If you said "south" to the above question, you are correct!

Write the direction you would be traveling for each set of cities. Use the four cardinal directions—north, south, east and west.

Atlanta to Los Angeles _____   Houston to Minneapolis _____

Seattle to Los Angeles _____   Miami to New York _____

San Francisco to Nashville_____   Detroit to New York _____

Denver to Salt Lake City_____   Boston to Minneapolis _____

Cincinnati to Detroit _____   Atlanta to Albuquerque _____

Chicago to Boston _____   Nashville to Miami _____

Locating Cities

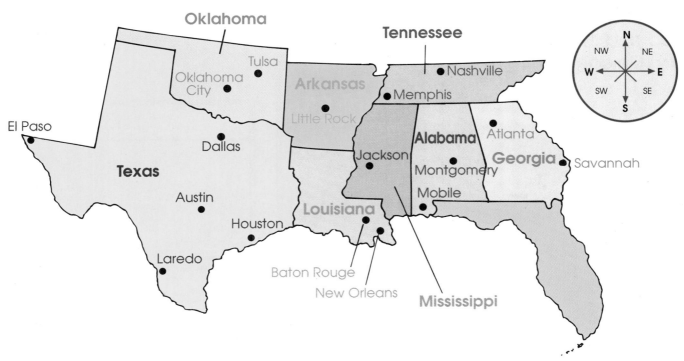

Directions: Use the compass rose to help you fill in each blank below with the correct direction.

1. El Paso, Texas, is _____ of Dallas, Texas.
2. Tulsa, Oklahoma, is _____ of Oklahoma City, Oklahoma.
3. Mobile, Alabama, is _____ of Baton Rouge, Louisiana.
4. Little Rock, Arkansas, is _____ of Nashville, Tennessee.
5. Houston, Texas, is _____ of New Orleans, Louisiana.
6. Jackson, Mississippi, is _____ of Memphis, Tennessee.
7. Dallas, Texas, is _____ of Austin, Texas.
8. The state of Louisiana is _____ of Arkansas.
9. The state of Alabama is _____ of Texas.
10. The state of Oklahoma is _____ of Tennessee.
11. The state of Georgia is _____ of Texas.
12. Atlanta, Georgia, is _____ of Savannah, Georgia.
13. The state of Tennessee is _____ of Arkansas.
14. Dallas, Texas, is _____ of Little Rock, Arkansas.
15. Mobile, Alabama, is _____ of Atlanta, Georgia.

Name: _____

How Many People?

This map uses symbols to show how many people live in each town. Use this map and the legend to answer the questions below.

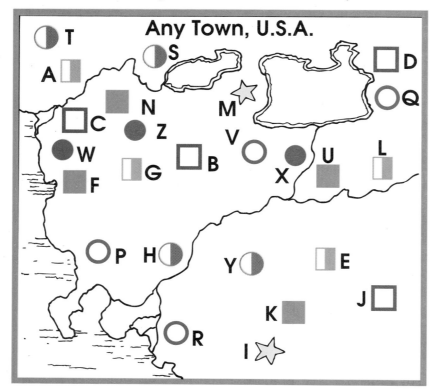

Legend	
	People
☐	0-500
◧	500-1,000
■	1,000-5,000
○	5,000-25,000
◖	25,000-50,000
●	50,000-100,000
☆	over 100,000

1. How many people live in a town that has this symbol ■ ? _____
2. What does ☆ mean on the map? _____
3. Name the four towns with 0-500 people. _____
4. How many towns have 1,000-5,000 people? _____
5. How many people live in town G? _____
6. Circle the town with the most people.   A   B   I
7. Circle the town with the fewest people.   L   K   J
8. Name the towns with 1,000-5,000 people. _____
9. How many towns have over 100,000 people? _____
10. Name the towns with 50,000-100,000 people. _____
11. Draw a circle around the towns with 500-1,000 people.
12. Draw a large **X** on the towns with 25,000-50,000 people.

Name: _____

What Is the Population?

Use this map of an imaginary state to answer the following questions.

Population Map

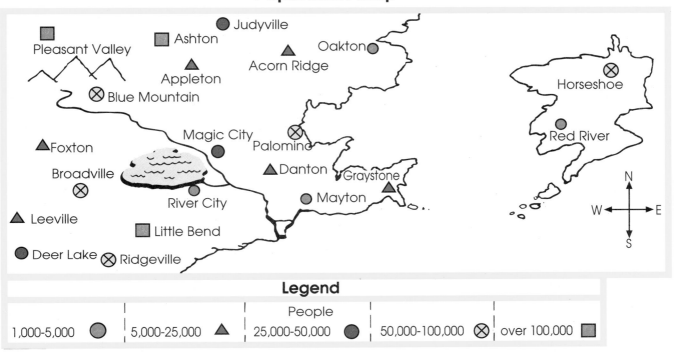

Legend

			People					
1,000-5,000 ⬤	5,000-25,000 ▲	25,000-50,000 ⬤	50,000-100,000 ⊗	over 100,000 ⬛

1. Name the five cities with a population of 50,000-100,000.

_____

2. Would you choose Foxton or Ashton for a baseball stadium which seats 50,000 people? _____

3. Name the three towns with a population over 100,000. _____

_____

4. Which is bigger—Pleasant Valley or Mayton? _____

5. Which town has more people—River City or Magic City? _____

6. Which town has more people—Judyville or Danton? _____

7. Which is larger—Little Bend or Ridgeville? _____

8. Which city is smaller—Blue Mountain or Deer Lake? _____

9. How many towns have 1,000-5,000 people? _____

10. How many towns have 5,000-25,000 people? _____

This page has been
intentionally left blank.

The Mole Family

A floor plan shows where things are placed in a room. The Mole Family has just had all of their new living room furniture delivered. Now they have to arrange it. Help them decide where to put each piece of furniture. Color and cut out the pictures of the furniture. Glue the pictures on the drawing of the Mole Family's living room to make a floor plan.

Mole Family's Floor Plan

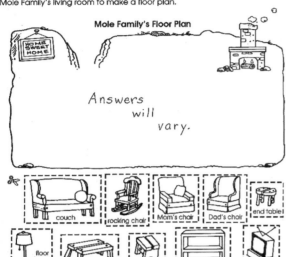

Answers will vary.

page 3

Prepare for the Show

It's the big event of the year! Old cars from all over the United States are being put on display. The boxes on the floor plan show the spaces where cars will be placed. Follow the directions on page 11 to complete the floor plan.

Car Display Floor Plan

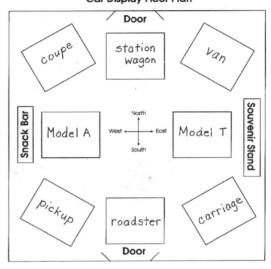

page 6

A Picture From Above

A floor plan looks like a picture someone drew looking down from the sky. It shows you where things are.

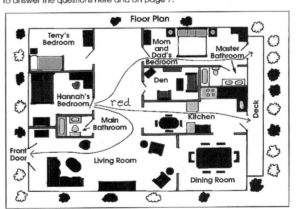

Circle the word which correctly completes each statement.
1. The TV is near the...   a. door   b. (window)   c. bed
2. The dresser is near the...   a. window   b. (door)   c. TV
3. Next to the bed is a...   a. TV   b. window   c. (table)
4. The bench is at the end of the...   a. (bed)   b. bookshelf   c. closet
5. The plant is by the...   a. dresser   b. bed   c. (bookshelf)
6. The bookshelf is next to the...   a. bed   b. closet   c. (door)
7. The lamp is on the...   a. (table)   b. TV   c. dresser

Follow these directions.
1. Draw a red circle around the TV.
2. Draw a black **X** on the desk.
3. Draw an oval rug in front of the bench using a color of your choice.
4. Draw a stuffed animal in the center of the bed.

Fill in these blanks with the correct word.
1. Between the closet and the TV is a _desk_.
2. The window is between the _plant_ and the TV.
3. When you walk in the door, the _dresser_ is to your right.
4. There (is)/are _one_ lamp(s) in the room.

page 5

Hannah's New House

Hannah's family just moved into a new house. It is very different from their other house. Hannah drew a floor plan of her new house. Use the floor plan to answer the questions here and on page 7.

Floor Plan

1. How many rooms does the house have? _nine_

2. Which room is the smallest? _Main Bathroom_

3. Which room is the largest? _Living Room_

page 9

Hannah's New House

4. Who has a room across from Mom and Dad's bedroom?
   Terry

5. Which rooms does Hannah walk past to go from the living room to her own bedroom?
   Main Bathroom, Kitchen

6. How many bedrooms are there? three

7. Which rooms have a door leading onto the deck?
   Kitchen, Mom and Dad's Bedroom

8. The front door opens into what room?
   Living Room

9. On the floor plan on page 6, use a red crayon to draw the routes Hannah could take from her room to a door leading outside in case of an emergency.

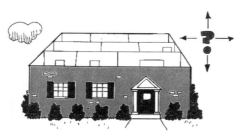

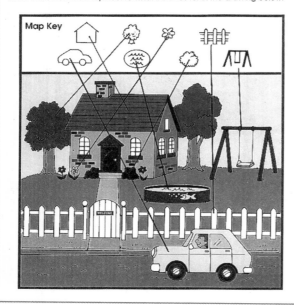

page 10

Symbols Replace Words

Symbols on a map show you where things are located.

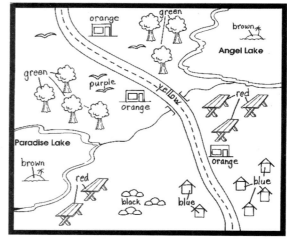

Directions: Use crayons or markers to complete the map.

1. Color the islands brown.
2. Color the trees green.
3. Color the rocks black.
4. Color the houses blue.
5. Color the stores orange.
6. Color the birds purple.
7. Color the picnic tables red.
8. Color the road yellow.

page 12

Symbols on Maps

A symbol is a picture that stands for something that is shown on a map. Symbols used in a map are shown in the Map Key. Look at the symbols. Draw a line from each symbol to what it stands for in the drawing below.

page 11

Kool Kids Mall

Mall Map

Directions: Use the key to locate the stores. Draw the following:

1. a red and blue sneaker in Silver Sneakers
2. a black musical note in the Music Stand
3. a pair of blue jeans in the Jeans Scene
4. a green tree on each side of the mall entrance
5. a red piece of pizza in the Snack Shack
6. a pair of eyes in the Video Arcade
7. a yellow book and a blue book in the Book Nook
8. an orange lollipop in the Candy Corner

page 13

Farmer Fritz

Map symbols can tell us how many of something there are. Each symbol can stand for 1 or any number of that item. This map shows Farmer Fritz's crops. Each vegetable or fruit stands for 1 plant. Use the map and key to answer the questions.

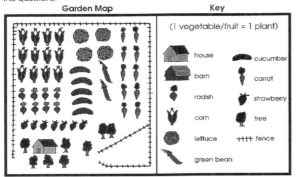

Garden Map

Key

(1 vegetable/fruit = 1 plant)

house   cucumber
barn   carrot
radish   strawberry
corn   tree
lettuce fence
green bean

1. How many plants of each vegetable does Farmer Fritz have?

radish __8__   cucumber __5__   corn __12__

carrot __10__   green bean __2__   lettuce __4__

2. What fruit did Farmer Fritz plant? __strawberries__

How many of these plants did he have? __7__

3. Farmer Fritz planted the most of which vegetable? __corn__

page 14

Take a Hike

This is a map showing three hiking trails.

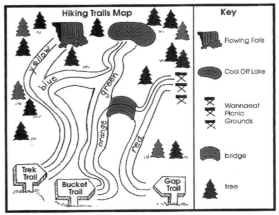

Hiking Trails Map

Key

Flowing Falls

Cool Off Lake

Wannaeat Picnic Grounds

bridge

tree

Directions:

1. Draw a red line along the trail that leads to the Wannaeat Picnic Grounds.

2. Draw a yellow line along the trail that leads to Flowing Falls.

3. Draw a green line along the trail that leads to Cool Off Lake.

4. Draw a blue line to show how you can go from Trek Trail to Cool Off Lake.

5. Draw an orange line to show how you can go from Bucket Trail to the Wannaeat Picnic Grounds.

page 16

Carmella's Candy

Carmella made a map of her candy store so that her customers could easily find their favorite candy. Use the map and key to answer the questions.

Candy Store Map

Key

(1 symbol = 2 boxes of candy)

chocolate chunks
cherry chocolates
licorice swirls
peanut clusters
cinnamon seashells
chewy dinosaurs
jelly beans
raspberry buttercreams

1. Each symbol equals how many boxes of candy? __2__

2. How many boxes of each kind of candy are there?

jelly beans __16__   licorice swirls __14__
chocolate chunks __12__   cherry chocolates __12__
peanut clusters __8__   chewy dinosaurs __4__
raspberry buttercreams __10__ cinnamon seashells __6__

3. Carmella has the greatest number of boxes of which candy?

__jellybeans__

page 15

Going from Place to Place

Some maps show you where places are located in a town.

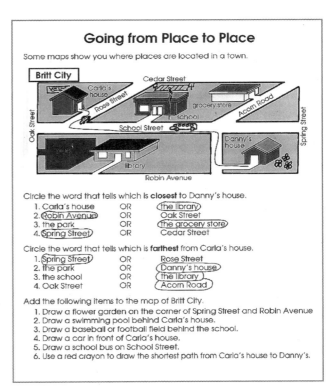

Britt City

Circle the word that tells which is **closest** to Danny's house.

1. Carla's house   OR   (the library)
2. (Robin Avenue)   OR   Oak Street
3. the park   OR   (the grocery store)
4. (Spring Street)   OR   Cedar Street

Circle the word that tells which is **farthest** from Carla's house.

1. (Spring Street)   OR   Rose Street
2. the park   OR   (Danny's house)
3. the school   OR   (the library)
4. Oak Street   OR   (Acorn Road)

Add the following items to the map of Britt City.

1. Draw a flower garden on the corner of Spring Street and Robin Avenue
2. Draw a swimming pool behind Carla's house.
3. Draw a baseball or football field behind the school.
4. Draw a car in front of Carla's house.
5. Draw a school bus on School Street.
6. Use a red crayon to draw the shortest path from Carla's house to Danny's.

page 17

Victory Celebration

Betsy, Rachel and Pat were so happy! They won their first baseball game. To celebrate, they wanted to have pizza and ice cream. Use this map and key to complete page 33.

Map

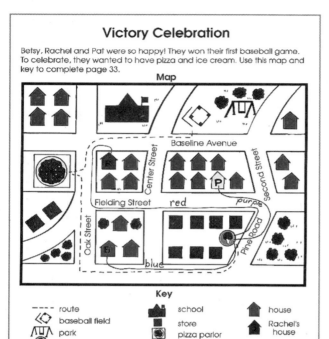

Key

- - - - route
◇ baseball field
ᴀᴧᴀ park
🏅 ice-cream shop
🌳 tree

🏫 school
🏬 store
🏪 pizza parlor
🏠 Betsy's house

🏠 house
🏠 Rachel's house
🅿 Pat's house

page 18

The Compass Rose

This is a compass rose. It tells the directions on a map. There are four arrows. Each arrow points in a different direction. These are called **cardinal** directions.

North
blue
West brown — green **East**
red
South

1. The arrow that points up is **north**. Color it blue.
2. The arrow that points down is **south**. Color it red.
3. The arrow that points to the right is **east**. Color it green.
4. The arrow that points to the left is **west**. Color it brown.

page 20

Victory Celebration

1. Use your finger to follow the route the girls took from the baseball field to the pizza parlor. On what street did they walk when they first left the baseball field?

    Baseline Avenue

2. Did they walk past the school? yes

3. Did they walk past a park? no

4. On what street is the pizza parlor? Oak Street

5. Use your finger to trace their route to the ice-cream shop. On what street is the ice-cream shop?

    Pine Road

6. Then, it was time to go home. Use a blue crayon to mark a route Betsy might have taken home.

7. Use a red crayon to mark a route Rachel might have taken home.

8. Use a purple crayon to mark a route Pat might have taken home.

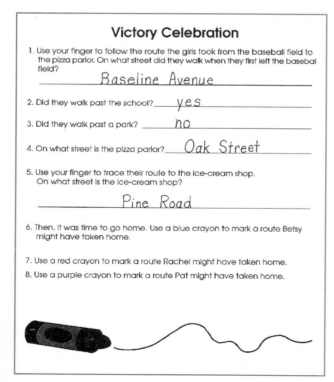

page 19

Pirate's Booty

Sedgewick the Pirate must be able to find his buried treasure when he returns to the island. Read the sentences. Write the words **north, south, east** and **west** in the blanks to help Sedgewick locate his treasure. Use the compass rose to help you.

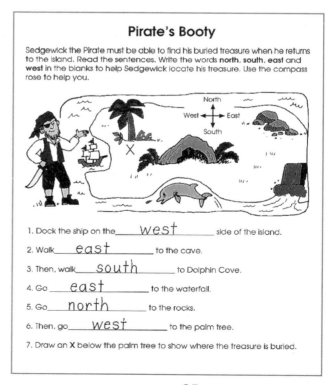

1. Dock the ship on the ___west___ side of the island.
2. Walk ___east___ to the cave.
3. Then, walk ___south___ to Dolphin Cove.
4. Go ___east___ to the waterfall.
5. Go ___north___ to the rocks.
6. Then, go ___west___ to the palm tree.
7. Draw an **X** below the palm tree to show where the treasure is buried.

page 21

What Do Hikers See?

Follow the directions to complete this area map.

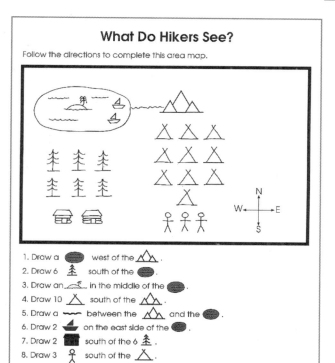

1. Draw a ⬭ west of the △△.
2. Draw 6 🌲 south of the ⬭.
3. Draw an ◠ in the middle of the ⬭.
4. Draw 10 △ south of the △△.
5. Draw a 〰 between the △△ and the ⬭.
6. Draw 2 ⛵ on the east side of the ⬭.
7. Draw 2 ▪ south of the 6 🌲.
8. Draw 3 🧍 south of the △△.

page 22

Space Ship Search

Gus Galactic needs help in identifying these alien spaceships. Write a ship's letter in each blank to solve these riddles.

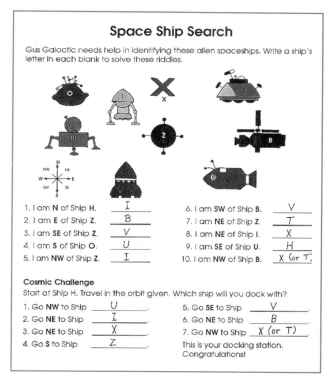

1. I am **N** of Ship **H.**   _I_
2. I am **E** of Ship **Z.**   _B_
3. I am **SE** of Ship **Z.**   _V_
4. I am **S** of Ship **O.**   _U_
5. I am **NW** of Ship **Z.**   _I_

6. I am **SW** of Ship **B.**   _V_
7. I am **NE** of Ship **Z.**   _T_
8. I am **NE** of Ship **I.**   _X_
9. I am **SE** of Ship **U.**   _H_
10. I am **NW** of Ship **B.**   _X (or T)_

Cosmic Challenge
Start at Ship H. Travel in the orbit given. Which ship will you dock with?

1. Go **NW** to Ship _U_ .
2. Go **NE** to Ship _I_ .
3. Go **NE** to Ship _X_ .
4. Go **S** to Ship _Z_ .

5. Go **SE** to Ship _V_ .
6. Go **NE** to Ship _B_ .
7. Go **NW** to Ship _X (or T)_ .

This is your docking station. Congratulations!

page 24

Dizzy Designers

Decorate the compass rose boxes by following the directions below.

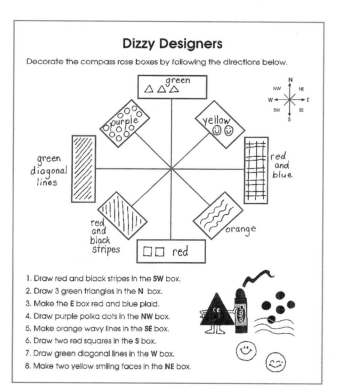

1. Draw red and black stripes in the **SW** box.
2. Draw 3 green triangles in the **N** box.
3. Make the **E** box red and blue plaid.
4. Draw purple polka dots in the **NW** box.
5. Make orange wavy lines in the **SE** box.
6. Draw two red squares in the **S** box.
7. Draw green diagonal lines in the **W** box.
8. Make two yellow smiling faces in the **NE** box.

page 23

Draw Your Own Map

A cartographer makes maps. Try your hand at being a cartographer and make your own map by following these directions. Read all directions before you begin.

1. Draw a compass rose using both cardinal and intermediate directions in the bottom right-hand corner of the map.
2. Draw a lake in the center of the map.
3. Northwest of the lake, draw some ducks in flight.
4. Directly south of the lake, draw six trees.
5. East of the ducks, draw the sun.
6. Southwest of the lake, draw a playground area.
7. East of the lake, draw a picnic area.

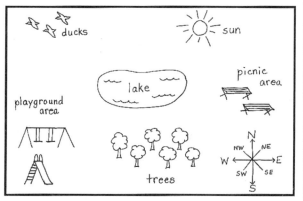

page 25

Legends Help You Read Maps

A legend is another word for a key. A map legend explains the symbols found in a map.

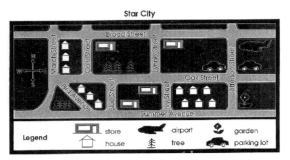

Directions: Use the legend box to answer the questions.

1. Does Star City have an airport? _yes_
2. How many houses are on Bird Avenue? _3_
3. What is on the corner of Oak Street and Jefferson Street? _parking lot_
4. The garden is on the corner of Jefferson Street and _Summer Avenue_.
5. How many stores are in Star City? _4_
6. What direction is Summer Avenue from Oak Street? _south_
7. Which street is directly west of Ivy Street? _Blue Street_
8. How many trees are north of Oak Street? _3_
9. How many houses are between Ivy Street and Jefferson Street? _6_
10. How many stores are north of Summer Avenue? _4_

page 26

North, South, East and West

You are flying in an airplane with the wind blowing sharply in your face. You are flying from Chicago to Nashville. In what direction are you traveling?

If you said "south" to the above question, you are correct!

Write the direction you would be traveling for each set of cities. Use the four cardinal directions—north, south, east and west.

Atlanta to Los Angeles _west_   Houston to Minneapolis _north_
Seattle to Los Angeles _south_   Miami to New York _north_
San Francisco to Nashville _east_   Detroit to New York _east_
Denver to Salt Lake City _west_   Boston to Minneapolis _west_
Cincinnati to Detroit _north_   Atlanta to Albuquerque _west_
Chicago to Boston _east_   Nashville to Miami _south_

page 28

Tourist Map of Oldtown

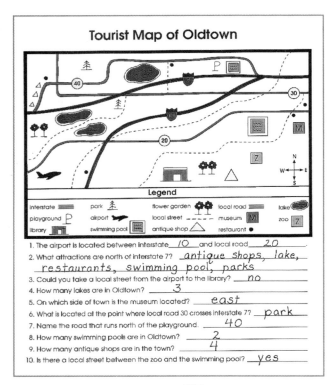

1. The airport is located between interstate _10_ and local road _20_.
2. What attractions are north of interstate 7? _antique shops, lake, restaurants, swimming pool, parks_
3. Could you take a local street from the airport to the library? _no_
4. How many lakes are in Oldtown? _3_
5. On which side of town is the museum located? _east_
6. What is located at the point where local road 30 crosses interstate 7? _park_
7. Name the road that runs north of the playground. _40_
8. How many swimming pools are in Oldtown? _2_
9. How many antique shops are in the town? _4_
10. Is there a local street between the zoo and the swimming pool? _yes_

page 27

Locating Cities

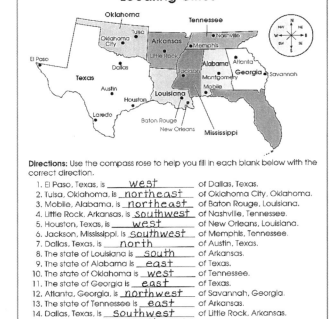

Directions: Use the compass rose to help you fill in each blank below with the correct direction.

1. El Paso, Texas, is _west_ of Dallas, Texas.
2. Tulsa, Oklahoma, is _northeast_ of Oklahoma City, Oklahoma.
3. Mobile, Alabama, is _northeast_ of Baton Rouge, Louisiana.
4. Little Rock, Arkansas, is _southwest_ of Nashville, Tennessee.
5. Houston, Texas, is _west_ of New Orleans, Louisiana.
6. Jackson, Mississippi, is _southwest_ of Memphis, Tennessee.
7. Dallas, Texas, is _north_ of Austin, Texas.
8. The state of Louisiana is _south_ of Arkansas.
9. The state of Alabama is _east_ of Texas.
10. The state of Oklahoma is _west_ of Tennessee.
11. The state of Georgia is _east_ of Texas.
12. Atlanta, Georgia, is _northwest_ of Savannah, Georgia.
13. The state of Tennessee is _east_ of Arkansas.
14. Dallas, Texas, is _southwest_ of Little Rock, Arkansas.
15. Mobile, Alabama, is _southwest_ of Atlanta, Georgia.

page 29

How Many People?

This map uses symbols to show how many people live in each town. Use this map and the legend to answer the questions below.

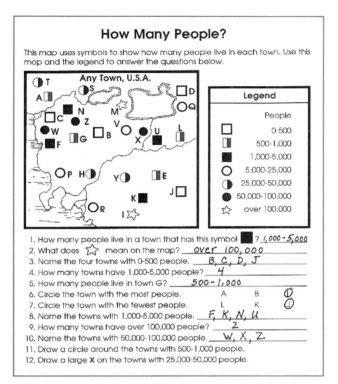

1. How many people live in a town that has this symbol ■? _1,000-5,000_
2. What does ☆ mean on the map? _over 100,000_
3. Name the four towns with 0-500 people. _B, C, D, J_
4. How many towns have 1,000-5,000 people? _4_
5. How many people live in town G? _500-1,000_
6. Circle the town with the most people. A B Ⓒ
7. Circle the town with the fewest people. L K Ⓙ
8. Name the towns with 1,000-5,000 people. _F, K, N, U_
9. How many towns have over 100,000 people? _2_
10. Name the towns with 50,000-100,000 people. _W, X, Z_
11. Draw a circle around the towns with 500-1,000 people.
12. Draw a large X on the towns with 25,000-50,000 people.

page 30

What Is the Population?

Use this map of an imaginary state to answer the following questions.

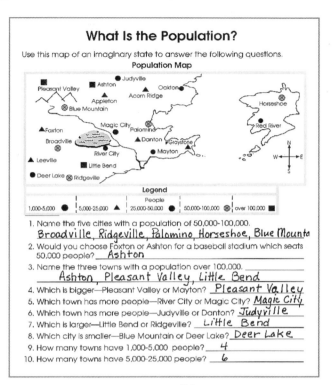

1. Name the five cities with a population of 50,000-100,000.
Broadville, Ridgeville, Palomino, Horseshoe, Blue Mounta
2. Would you choose Foxton or Ashton for a baseball stadium which seats 50,000 people? _Ashton_
3. Name the three towns with a population over 100,000. _Ashton, Pleasant Valley, Little Bend_
4. Which is bigger—Pleasant Valley or Mayton? _Pleasant Valley_
5. Which town has more people—River City or Magic City? _Magic City_
6. Which town has more people—Judyville or Danton? _Judyville_
7. Which is larger—Little Bend or Ridgeville? _Little Bend_
8. Which city is smaller—Blue Mountain or Deer Lake? _Deer Lake_
9. How many towns have 1,000-5,000 people? _4_
10. How many towns have 5,000-25,000 people? _6_

page 31